T0085940

The Poems
of Alexander
Lawrence Posey

The Poems of Alexander Lawrence Posey

Alexander Lawrence Posey

MINT EDITIONS

The Poems of Alexander Lawrence Posey was first published in 1910.

This edition was published by Mint Editions in 2023.

Print ISBN 9781513201047   E ISBN 9781513127965

Published by Mint Editions

 MINT
EDITIONS

MintEditionBooks.com

Publishing Director: Jennifer Newens
Design & Production: Rachel Lopez Metzger
Project Manager: Micaela Clark
Typesetting: Hazel Risner

Contents

THE MEMOIR OF
ALEXANDER LAWRENCE POSEY

I

ALEXANDER LAWRENCE POSEY
WAS A CREEK INDIAN

He was a poet of the first order, a humorist, a philosopher, a man of affairs. He achieved fame as an English-Indian dialect writer and journalist. He was the leading man of the Creeks and the one great man produced by the Confederacy known as the Five Civilized Tribes.

Posey was born in what is now McIntosh County, Oklahoma, eight miles west of Eufaula, August 3, 1873. He was accidentally drowned in the North Canadian river, near Eufaula, May 27, 1908.

Posey's father was Lewis H. Posey, a Scotch-Irish native of the Indian Territory, who claimed to be one-sixteenth Creek blood. The elder Posey was born in the Creek country about the year 1841, and, his parents having died when he was a child, he was reared by a Creek woman who lived near Fort Gibson. It is quite probable that he had no Indian blood, for his children are officially enrolled as of half Creek blood by the Dawes Commission. His parents wandered into the Creek country from Texas, and little is now known of them. He was a jolly, mirth-loving man, who never lost an opportunity to perpetrate a practical joke. For some time he was a Deputy U.S. Marshal at Fort Smith. After his marriage to a Creek girl he established himself on a large ranch at Bald Hill, up the Canadian some eight miles west of Eufaula, where he lived until his death. He is said to have been the only white man of his time who could speak the Creek language perfectly. He attended a school taught by one Lewis Robertson, and there learned to read and write English, and he secured some knowledge of arithmetic. He is said to have been rather unruly at school, and it is related that when Robertson went away to get married he left his school in charge of Mrs. Mary Herod. She found it necessary to bring Posey up to the front and seat him where she could have an eye on him all the time, it being otherwise impossible to maintain any semblance of order in the school.

The mother of the poet is still living. She is the daughter of Pohos Harjo, but her English name was Nancy Phillips. She is a Creek of full and pure blood. She belongs to the Wind Clan, the strongest clan of the Creeks, and is a member of the Tuskegee Town or Band of the Muscogee Nation. She was married to Lewis H. Posey about October, 1872, when but fifteen years old. Her famous son was born when she was in her seventeenth year.

The Harjo family is noted as one of big warriors, and is the oldest of the Muskogees or Creeks. It was also the largest as far back as we have any knowledge of this people, the tribal census of 1832 showing almost one-fourth of the tribe as members of it. This proportion diminished up to the time of making the final rolls, but even these show the family to be very large.

It is recorded of Mrs. Posey that she was a devoted mother, as most Indian women are. She gave her whole time to the comfort of her family, and saw to it that her children had at all times an abundance of wholesome food.

If there was little left from the midday meal she would often bake an extra pan of bread, that they might have all they wished to eat until supper was served. She was a tidy housekeeper, and the dirt supposed to be indigenous to an Indian dwelling was not to be found in her home. She was careful of her personal appearance, and had the Indian fondness for decided colors. In hot weather she would frequently put cold water on her head and the heads of her children, believing it a protection from extreme heat. She is a very sincere and devout Christian and a member of the Baptist Church. Once she was in the house of a white woman who was dying, and who requested that someone should pray for her. Mrs. Posey offered the prayer, speaking in her own tongue, and those present always remembered the earnestness and eloquence of her appeal for the dying woman.

Concerning his parents I find this written by Posey:

"I was born near Eufaula, in the Creek Nation, Indian Territory, August 3, 1873. Both my parents were Creek Indians, but they belonged to different clans, my father being a Broken Arrow, and my mother a Tuskegee. My father also possessed a percentage of Scotch-Irish blood, but my mother is a pure-blood Creek Indian. My grandparents came from Alabama, the former home of the Creek people. My father was a self-educated man of uncommon intelligence, with a philosophical and scientific turn of mind, while my mother, though uneducated and unable to speak a word of English, is a woman of rare native sense."

The statement that "Broken Arrow" and "Tuskegee" are the names of clans in the Creek social organization is a slip of the pen of the poet. He had in mind the "Bands" or "Towns" into which the tribe is divided for the purposes of civil government. And I am satisfied that his father had no Indian blood.

II

Of these parents came the poet. He seems to have been a child of deep feeling, very quick and accurate observation, and often self-conscious and reflective. He was sensitive and reticent and an enthusiastic lover of nature—streams, hills, prairies, trees, flowers, birds, animals, the tangled wildwood, the heavens at night, and the magnificent cloud-displays seen in his native land. But, with all these, he was a genuine boy. From his father he had inherited a sense of humor and a love for practical jokes. He was in much innocent mischief from the time he could run about, and as the good old law of punishment for disobedience was in vogue in the Posey household, few months passed that did not bring him a whipping. This punishment was administered in a proper spirit and was wholesome correction. The boy was not humiliated, nor was the natural inclination of his mind repressed. He was never stubborn or unreasonable, and resentment and malice were not in him. If his dress became soiled the least bit he would cry for a clean one.

The companion of the poet's childhood and youth was Tom, a full-blood Creek boy, an orphan taken into the Posey home and reared as one of the family. Once Mrs. Posey set these boys to work in the garden. After directing them as to their task she went into the house, saying that she would return in due time to see what progress they made. Instead of bending to their work they spent the time in digging a hole in the garden-path, which they covered over with small sticks and earth. When Mrs. Posey returned she fell into this hole, to the great amusement of the thoughtless and mischief-loving lads. But there was a stout paling fence about the garden, and they could not escape; they were caught and soundly whipped.

On another occasion when she had put them to some task, which they went about with that deliberation which marks the labor of boys on the old homestead, she remarked that they moved about as though they had stones tied on their backs. Here was a suggestion. When she had gone back into the house the boys went to the bam-lot and spent the time until her reappearance tying stones on their backs and carrying them about.

For summer wear Mrs. Posey made the boys a single flowing garment which reached to the heels. Memory of these remained with the poet, and in afteryears he said of them:

"It is enough to say, concerning my youth, that I was raised on a farm and was accounted a pretty weedy crop. The cockle-burrs and crab-grass grew all the more prolifically after I had been given a good thrashing. Tom, an orphan boy adopted by my father, was my youth-long companion, and I often look back to the 'days of the lost sunshine,' when we romped in our long shirts, or 'sweeps,' as we called them, which my mother fashioned for our use. These shirts or 'sweeps' were long, flowing garments, made on the order of a tunic, but longer and more dignified. There was a vast freedom in these gowns; freedom for the wind to play in, and they were so easily thrown aside at the 'old swimmin' hole.' We looked forward with regret to the time when we would have to discard them for jeans, coats and trousers and copper-toed boots, though these were desirable to chase rabbits in on a snowy day. Those who have never worn 'sweeps' have never known half of the secrets whispered by the winds of boyhood."

Until he was some twelve years old Posey spoke only Creek, the language of his mother. Like her, he could understand English fairly well, but its construction was so entirely different from his native tongue that he feared to trust himself in the use of it. The Indian is extremely sensitive to ridicule, and this often prevents his efforts to speak the language of the white man; and this is especially true of Indian women. They, and sometimes the men, will pretend to an ignorance of English and sit taciturn and unresponsive when addressed in that language, though they may understand it perfectly and speak it fairly. That Posey so mastered a language which may be said to have been alien to him that he wrote readily and elegantly its most difficult form of composition, is a mark of the genius of the man. His first use of English was compelled by his father, and is thus described by him:

"My first teacher was a dried-up, hard-up, weazen-faced, irritable little fellow, with an appetite that caused the better dishes on my father's table to disappear rapidly. My father picked him up somewhere, and seeing that he had a bookish turn, gave him a place in our family as a private teacher. From him I learned the alphabet and to read short sentences, but I never spoke any English until I was compelled to speak it by my father. One evening, when I blurted out in the best Creek I could command, and began telling him about a horse-hunt, he cut me off shortly: 'Look here, young man, if you don't tell me that in English, after supper I am going to wear you out.' I was hungry, but this put an abrupt end to my desire for the good things I had heaped on my plate.

I got up from the table and made myself useful—brought water from the well, turned the cows into the pasture—thinking maybe this would cause him to forget what he had said. My goodness, however, was without avail, for as soon as he came from the table he asked me in a gentle but firm voice to relate my horse-hunt. Well, he was so pleased with my English that he never afterward allowed me to speak Creek."

Here we have the account of Posey's first experience with a teacher and the progress he made, which was limited enough. But it must not be supposed that he had learned nothing of worth in his childhood. His mother is familiar with all the mythology and folklore of the Creeks. She is far above the average in intelligence, and as a storyteller she is unsurpassed by any of her people. Sitting about the blazing fagots in the open fireplace on the long evenings of winter, she told her children all the legends of the Creeks,—their migrations, their simple and happy life in the primitive forests before it was contaminated by the vices of the white man, their proud tribal history of the days when they were free men and lords of the earth, creation myths, ghost and fairy stories,—all the lore of an ancient and imaginative people.

It all depends on who hears a story. The old parable of the sower is the law of the intellect—most of the seed falls on stony ground and brings forth nothing. A little falls on fertile soil and yields increase an hundred fold. To the sensitive mind of this Indian boy these tales of ancient days revealed a new world, peopled with characters as fascinating and fantastic as any Shakespeare ever saw in the magic realms of his creation. Had not death intervened, these would sometime have stood before us in the matchless array and imagery of genius. Even as it was, they stirred the soul of this Creek boy and became the inspiration of that delicate perception of nature's charms which he has recorded for us.

III

Posey did not begin to discover himself until he was sent to the Indian University (Baptist), at Bacone, in the suburbs of Muskogee. This school was founded in 1880, for the training of native young men and women for Christian work among the Indian people. A. C. Bacone was its president and its moving spirit. Young Posey was sent there in 1890—when he was seventeen. He was then a reserved and timid boy, with no thought whatever of the possibilities he possessed. Under the direction of President Bacone, Posey soon began to take good rank in the life and work of the University. He describes his life there very briefly, saying:

> "When I was old enough to leave home my father sent me to a public school at Eufaula, where I learned enough to enable me to enter a second academic grade at the Indian University. I remained there about five years. During my stay at the University I acted as librarian on Sundays. I set type after school hours on weekdays for a little paper called the *Instructor*, published by the faculty."

Some copies of *The B.I.U. Instructor* have come into my hands. The paper was a monthly four-column folio, eleven by fourteen inches in size. M. L. Brown and C. H. Maxon were the editors, and the first number of the paper must have been published in October, 1891. Not only did Posey set type on this paper, but his first literary efforts to see the light were published in it. These were usually, but not always, in verse. In the number for October, 1892, he published "The Comet's Tale," a poem of near three columns, which gives the Indian tradition of the appearance of a great comet previous to the coming of the ships of the white men to discover America.

It is no inferior production, though not at all equal to his later work. In the number for December, 1892, he published "The Indian: What of Him?" an optimistic article in prose. Also "The Sea God," an Indian legend, in verse. In the January, 1894, number appeared his "Death of a Window Plant," the first of his poems to attract more than local attention. This was published far and wide, with comments most flattering to the young poet. In the following March the *Instructor* contained "The River Strange," a poem of some merit, and "Fixico Yahola's Revenge," the story of a warrior who assumed the form of a bear.

The numbers mentioned above are all that I have seen of the *Instructor*, and judging from the contents of those it is safe to say that Posey wrote much for the paper. At the time of his graduation (in 1895) he was well known to all the people of the Five Civilized Tribes, and he was in great favor with his own people.

IV

When Posey left school he entered Creek politics. In September, 1895, he was elected to a seat in the House of Warriors, the popular branch of the Creek Legislature. He was sent a delegate to every council or conclave convened in the Indian Territory to discuss the status or policy of the Indians or to take concerted action in their interest.

V

In 1896 Posey was Superintendent of the Creek Orphan Asylum at Okmulgee. It was in this year that he was married. Of this event I find the following entry in his Journal, under date of January 4, 1897:

"I have nowhere mentioned my 'better half.' The story of our courtship and marriage would make a readable romance. I was introduced to her one morning, nearly two years ago, by J. N. Thornton, 'ye' editor of the *Indian Journal*, at breakfast in a hotel at Eufaula. The beauty of the young school-teacher thoroughly charmed me; and, though I saw her frequently, I could not sufficiently overcome my Indian nature to talk with her. She went away. I thought of her constantly; would sometimes grow anxious to declare my love by letter. Two months passed, and she returned to take up her work. One day I made it convenient to pass the schoolhouse. I got a glimpse of her as I hurried by on 'Ballie,' and another as I returned. My love grew deeper. Three months later I was elected to the position I now hold. One night I was at Eufaula, and by chance met her. I offered her a place in my school; she accepted it, and, when summer was come again, 'two hearts beat as one.'"

The young lady was Miss Minnie Harris, of Fayetteville, Arkansas, and the wedding was on the 9th of May, 1896. Concerning her acquaintance with Posey and her marriage to him, Mrs. Posey wrote me as follows:

"I met Mr. Posey in Eufaula, in July, 1895. I saw little of him, though, until in January, 1896, when I was employed by him to act as Matron of the Creek Orphan Home at Okmulgee. He would read to me, and he asked my opinion of all that he wrote. He also was fond of having me read to him, or him to me, evenings, discussing the things we read,—mostly poems. Mr. Posey spent most of the forenoons in his study, but often in the afternoons he would ask me to accompany him in his walks and drives. I think he admired me for my practical ways. I saved him much bother and vexation over details in looking after the school."

Posey remained in charge of the Orphan Asylum until October, 1897, when he resigned. In the following December he was appointed Superintendent of Public Instruction of the Creek (or Muscogee) Nation, but he wished to put in cultivation his farm, which consists of several hundred acres, and so he soon resigned that office. From Okmulgee he moved to his farm, near Stidham, Oklahoma, and near that of his father, on which he had been born and reared.

VI

From the time of his marriage, in May, 1896, to October, 1897, Posey wrote many of his best poems. When he moved to his farm he continued his literary work. There he passed the golden era of his life. Mrs. Posey assumed the management of the farm—no small matter, as there were a number of tenants to reckon with. She never allowed him to be disturbed in his work, in which he was rather slow and very cautious. He had a small select library—all favorite books—which he read much, as reference to his Journal shows. He did his best literary work here. He would stroll about the farm in the afternoons to observe the squirrels and birds. He had a number of pet squirrels which interested him much. He was fond of dogs, and had a number of them. He even made a pet of a large turkey-gobbler, which soon became a terror to strangers and to the other pets. He had fine flowers growing about the premises, and these he loved to water and tend. He spent some time almost every day talking to droll characters who lived in the neighborhood, and to old men and women of his tribe.

Posey had great reverence and love for his mother, and visited her frequently. He never failed to spend the Christmas season with her. Her other children were not so thoughtful of her comfort, and after the death of her husband she was often lonely. She almost worshipped her gifted son, and his homecoming was her joy. In their conversations with others he would interpret what was being said if he thought she did not fully comprehend all that was spoken in English.

But Posey could not be permitted to remain in pastoral peace on the Canadian. He had fine executive ability, and was the most learned man of all the Creeks. The National High School at Eufaula was in need of competent management, and his government urged him to accept the superintendency of it, which he finally did, though with much reluctance. At Eufaula he was importuned constantly for contributions of poems and sketches for the *Indian Journal*, published there. He always complied with these requests when he found it possible to do so, and here he began to be interested in newspaper work.

When Posey had put the administration of affairs at the Eufaula High School on a satisfactory basis he was urged to do the same for the Wetumpka National School, which he finally consented to do. But he was never a lover of official position, and he did not remain long at Wetumpka. He returned to Eufaula and took editorial charge of the *Indian Journal*.

VII

It was as editor of the *Indian Journal* that Posey began the production of those articles which permanently fixed his fame in literature. The Dawes Commission was then closing up the affairs of the Five Civilized Tribes. An era of graft and plunder began, the likes of which has not been seen in America. The Indians became the prey of unprincipled lawyers and scoundrels of the lowest order. These plied their nefarious business openly and with brazen assurance. Much plundering was done with the knowledge and sanction of Federal officials, high and low. Millions were stolen through the medium of townsites. The Indians were conscious of the debauch of which they were the victims, but they were utterly helpless. Posey sought indirectly to call attention to what his people were suffering. Whether he accomplished his design is doubtful. But in his humorously satirical letters he developed an entirely new field in literature. To that time it had been supposed that the Indian was incapable of humorous conceptions. It was believed that he was too grim and stoical to perceive any facetious allusions to himself or others. These letters were continued irregularly for some years, and in an English-Indian dialect dealt with those events which were rapidly displacing the Indian in his native land. They purported to be conversations between Wolf Warrior, Hot Gun, Kono Harjo, and Tookpofko Micco,—old Creeks. Some of the prominent men in the affairs of Oklahoma in that day were spoken of by these names: Tams Bixby was "Tarns Big Pie." Pliny Soper was "Plenty-so-far." Secretary Hitchcock was "Secretary Its-cocked." Governor Haskell was "Governor C. N. Has-it." Senator Owen was "Col. Robert L. Owes-em." These letters were copied by the press of the entire country, and enjoyed by appreciative readers from Maine to California. Reference is here made to "The Fus Fixico Letters" only as an incident in the literary fame of Posey. It is the design of the present editor to prepare them for the press and have them issued in a separate volume at some time in the future if times are propitious.

VIII

Posey edited the *Indian Journal* a little more than two years. His growing fame tended to draw him to Muskogee, the metropolis of the Indian country. Man offers came to him from people and institutions of that town, and finally he and Ira L. Reeves took charge of the *Muskogee Times*. However, that venture did not prove to be satisfactory to him. There was much work to be done by the United Indian Agency which only a man familiar with every phase of Indian life and character could do, and Posey was induced to take a place in the Agency. But at this time knowledge of his influence and ability came to the Dawes Commission, which was in need of some one with exactly his qualifications. In each of the tribes were many Indians who refused to accept their allotments of land and surrender their tribal authority. These, in the Creek tribe, were followers of Chief Crazy Snake. Posey saw the inevitable. He realized that the Indians were helpless. If any Indian failed to take his allotment the tribal land would be disposed of without much consideration for his interest. If he could be prevailed on to accept his land he could be allotted that on which he lived and had improved; otherwise his farm would go to any who might choose to have it allotted to himself. There were many "lost Indians"—those who had married into other tribes, or who had wandered away to live in secluded and solitary places, as is the manner of Indians. These were to be found and enrolled. And there were the Creek babies born after the original rolls had been closed; they were to be sought out and enrolled. Posey was prevailed on to undertake this work. The principal consideration with him was that he could do much good for his people in the work so necessary to be done. He was furnished a stenographer and told to go about his duties in his own way. I find in his Journal this reference to his taking the field in this pursuit:

> "Drennon C. Skaggs and myself constitute what is officially known as the 'Creek Enrollment Field Party of the Commission to the Five Civilized Tribes.' I am Clerk in Charge and Creek Interpreter, with Skaggs acting as Notary Public and stenographer. Our business is to secure additional evidence in applications for enrollment, search for 'lost Creeks' and conciliate the 'Snakes.' We were detailed for this work in October of last year; and though we have labored steadily and strenuously ever since, the end is not yet. There is

more evidence to be secured, more 'lost Creeks' to be found, and more 'Snakes' to be conciliated. This work cannot be accomplished in the office of the Commission at Muscogee—'lost Creeks' do not turn up there to be identified—the 'Snakes' will not be coaxed in to establish better relations with the Government—important witnesses in citizenship cases pending before the Commission cannot go to Muskogee at their own expense for the purpose of testifying—the work must be done on the roadside, at the hearthside, and in the cotton-patch. Hence the 'Creek Enrollment Field Party.'

The so-called 'lost Creeks' are persons whose names appear on the tribal rolls, but none of whom the Commission has been able to identify. These people, of course, cannot be allowed to participate in the distribution of tribal property until their identify has been established and their rights as citizens determined according to law.

The 'Snakes,' so called because of their leader, Crazy Snake, are a faction of the Creeks who are opposed to the allotment of lands in severalty and the relinquishment of tribal authority. They number several hundred, and were arbitrarily allotted lands by the Commission. They have persistently ignored the work of the Commission and refused to be governed by its decrees. They wish to live in undisturbed enjoyment of their old customs and usages and rights guaranteed to them by former treaties with th e Government."

To show the painstaking care with which he performed his duties I give here one deposition taken by Posey:

C. I. 3177.
EN. 986.
EN. 764.

In the matter of the application for the enrollment of
Honechike, Cosarpe, Itshas Harjo, Marley, Liley, Mewike, Polly,
Mary, Tissie, Warsarsie, Hoekapo, Sallie, Lydia and Alexander, as
citizens by blood of the Creek Nation.

ITSHAS JARHO, being first duly sworn by and
examined through Alex Posey, Notary Public and official
interpreter, testified as follows:

By the Commissioner.

Q. What is your name?
A. Itshas Harjo.

Q. Are you known by any other name?
A. I am commonly known among my Cherokee brethren
as Old Creek Beaver, but my real name is Itshas Harjo.

Q. How old are you?
A. I have passed through many days and traveled a long
way, the shadows have fallen all about me and I can see
but dimly, but my mind is dear and my memory has not
failed me. I cannot count the years I have lived. All that I
know about my age is that I was old enough to draw the
bow and kill squirrels at the time of the second emigration
of the Creeks and Cherokees from the old country under
the leadership of Chief Cooweescoowee. I was born near
Eufaula, Alabama, and left there when about fifteen years
of age. I was about sixteen years old when I arrived in this
country, the peaches were green when we left Alabama
and the wild onions were plentiful here when we arrived.

Q. What is your post office address?
A. Bunch; but the mail I have received through that office
has not been of a kind to please me, the same being official
communications from the United States Government
relative to the allotment of land.

Q. Are you a citizen of the Creek Nation?
A. I am a full-blood Creek Indian, but I have never lived

in the Creek Nation.

Q. Were you ever enrolled as a citizen of the Creek Nation?
A. Yes, sir; once upon a time before the war I drew money at a per capita payment made at Old Norfolk Town, in the Creek Nation, but I have never participated in any Creek payment since.

Q. Did you not draw money as a member of Ketchapataka Town when the last Creek per capita payment was made, in 1895?
A. No, sir; as I have told you, I drew money only once in the Creek Nation, and that was before the war.

Q. On the 1895 Tribal roll of the Creek Nation of Ketchapataka Town are found the names of Honechike, Cosarpe, Itshas Harjo, Marley, Liley, and Mewike, and there is an application pending before the Commissioner to the Five Civilized Tribes for the enrollment as citizens of the Creek Nation of the persons whose names appear in this list. Does the Itshas Harjo in this list refer to you?
A. Evidently—because Marley, Liley and Mewike are my relatives; but we do not belong to Ketchapataka Town, and if our names appear upon the roll of that town they were erroneously put there. The town to which we belong is Arbeka Deep Fork.

Q. Who are Honechike and Cosarpe, appearing in this list with you?
A. Honechike was an old Creek woman who used to live among the Cherokees; she returned to the Creek Nation many years ago and died there. I cannot account for Cosarpe; I never heard the name before.

Q. What relation is Marley, Liley, and Mewike to you?
A. Mewike was a brother of mine, who died in March of last year. Marley and Liley are my nieces, being the daughters of my brother Mewike. Marley died about two years ago, and only Liley is now living. My brother was variously known as Mewike, Ewike, and John Killer. Marley was sometimes called Meheley, and Liley is also known as Tahkee.

Q. Do you know if they have been enrolled and allotted land as Cherokees?
A. I think they are enrolled as Cherokees, but I am not sure.

Q. Where was your brother living at the time of his death?
A. In Saline District.

Q. Had he always lived in the Cherokee Nation?
A. Yes, sir.

Q. Was never a resident of the Creek Nation?
A. No, sir.

Q. Have you resided continuously in the Cherokee Nation ever since your removal from Alabama?
A. Yes, sir; I have lived in the hollows of these hills ever since I established a home for myself, and you are the first Creek-speaking stranger that has visited me on my own premises. If I had met you out in the woods I would have spoken Cherokee to you and you would not have known that I was a Creek Indian.

Q. Are you enrolled as a citizen of the Cherokee Nation?
A. If I am I do not know it. I have not been curious enough to inquire into that matter.

Q. Then you do not know whether an allotment of land has been set aside to you as a Cherokee or not?
A. No, sir; I have never filed upon any land. I am opposed to the allotment of land among the Indians. If my name appears upon either the Creek or Cherokee roll, and for that reason I am to be hedged about with comer-stones, I want it stricken from the roll.

Q. On the 1895 Tribal roll of the Creek Nation, Weogufke Town, are found the following names: Polly, Mary, Tissie, Warsarsie, Hoekapo, Sallie, and Lydia. Do you know any such persons?
A. Yes, sir; Polly was a Creek woman, who died about twenty-five years ago. Tissie is a son of Hully and Polly, who died many years ago; his parents were both Creeks. Tissie is living, and is known both as Chissie and John Simmons. Warsarsie is a first cousin of Tissie; he is living, and is also known as Charles Rogers. Hoekapo is a brother of Tissie; he is also living, and is sometimes known as

George Simmons. Sallie is a sister of Tissie and Hoekapo; she is living, and is now the wife of my grandson, Clem Beaver. Lydia was a sister of Sallie; she died in 1903.

Q. Do you know if any of these people were enrolled as Cherokee Nation?
A. I have heard that they were enrolled as Cherokees, but I do not know it to be true of my own knowledge.

Q. Do you know Alexander, whose name appears upon the Creek Tribal roll as a member of Okfuske Deep Fork Town?
A. Yes, sir. He is now dead. He was known as Alex Sunday here, and had been given land as a Cherokee when he died.

Q. When did he die?
A. January 1, 1903, and is buried in a graveyard near here.

Q. Who were his parents?
A. Wechus Harjo, of Okfuske Deep Fork, was his father, and Lizzie Harjo, of Topofka Town, was his mother.

J. B. Myers, being first duly sworn, states, that as stenographer to the Commissioner to the Five Civilized Tribes he recorded the testimony in the foregoing proceedings, and that the above is a true and correct transcript of his stenographic notes thereof.

[Seal.]

(Signed) J. B. Myers.

Subscribed and sworn to before me, this 17th day of January, 1907.

(Signed) Alex Posey.

IX

When the people of the Indian Territory realized that single statehood was inevitable, they saw that it was necessary for them to take some action which would enable their section of the coming commonwealth to act in concert and thereby secure for it an equal influence in public affairs. It was decided that this could be best accomplished by an effort to secure statehood for the Indian Territory. A constitutional convention was therefore called to meet at Muskogee, August 21, 1905. Of this body Posey was made the Secretary. An excellent constitution was formulated, and its simple, terse, clear English was principally the work of Posey. He proposed Sequoyah as the name of the Indian State, and it was adopted,—a fitting tribute to the famous Cherokee and one of the greatest men that ever lived. Single statehood came, as the Indians had foreseen, and the unification of thought and purpose of the people of the Indian Territory accomplished all for which the convention had been called. The control of the new State was completely wrested from old Oklahoma. The result was a great tribute to the statesmanship of Posey and General Pleasant Porter, Chief of the Creeks, for they mainly originated the movement for the State of Sequoyah, and did much to make it the success it afterward proved.

X

When the work of the Dawes Commission was completed in the particular field in which Posey was employed, he thought to return to Eufaula and buy the *Indian Journal*. Statehood had come, and the tribes had been broken on the wheel and ground to powder. Posey's home was near Eufaula. There, too, was the old homestead where he was born and where his ancestors were buried. To n o other people does sentiment so appeal as to the Indians, and it was one of the considerations which inclined Posey to return to the Canadian. Then, a new era had come for the Indian. It was required of him that he abandon communal life and try to live as an individual unit of society. Posey felt the change, though he was confident of his ability to acquit himself well in the new order of things. His knowledge of the country and his people would enable him to deal honorably and successfully in lands and timber, in oil, natural gas, and coal. In furtherance of these designs he made his connections for future business at Muskogee, and set out for Eufaula. Alas! It was a fatal journey! I shall permit one who was his companion and who came near death in the same catastrophe to tell of it:

Story Of Posey's Death As Told By Attorney R. D. Howe.

R. D. Howe, the attorney who accompanied Alex Posey when drowned, made the following statement to the *Times-Democrat*.

"So much as been said and written, and so many have come to Mrs. Alex Posey with different stories in regard to the death of her husband, that I take it upon myself, being with him and an eye-witness to his death, to write the true story of this sad occurrence.

On the morning of the 27th day of May, 1908, Alex Posey and myself started for the town of Eufaula on the morning passenger, to close up some business we had with each other in the county court. When the train had passed the town of Wells, or Cathey, it stopped, and in a few minutes began to back to the siding at the town of Wells; here Alex and myself got off, and walking down to the front of the engine, met the conductor and some other railroad men who had just come from down the track in the direction of the river. We both stepped up and asked the conductor if he was going on to Eufaula. His reply was 'no,' as there was a small washout in the track down this side of the river, and though it was not enough to keep a man from crossing yet it would be dangerous for the engine to cross the place. Just at that time another railroad man stepped up and told us that the dirt was washed out from under five or six ties, but that any man could walk across them, and added that it was only about three miles to the town of Eufaula. Alex then turned to me and said in a joking way: 'Bob, if you will help me carry my grip, we will walk to the town.' My reply was, 'Come ahead,' and we then started down the track, but just before starting the train pulled out and left us standing on the road-crossing. When we got down the track about a half-mile we could see the water up on the track, and on Alex saying that he was afraid to go down too close, as the water might take the track out, I replied that I would go down and see the men who were with us wade through, and if it was not deep we could wade it as they did. In a few minutes these men came back and said that they had gotten to a place that they could not wade, but if they had a boat they could easily row around the place. I asked them how wide it was, and they said about ten or fifteen feet. Alex then turned to a negro sitting there and asked him if he knew where we could get a boat. His reply was that he had one, and he would go and get it and row us around this bad place in the road.

This was about eight o'clock in the morning. While the negro was getting the boat, Alex and myself went up to a farmhouse to get our breakfast, and while sitting there I told him I had had my breakfast early in the morning at home. He then said to me: 'As you have had your breakfast, you go and see if that negro has gotten back with the boat, and don't let the other men get it.' I then got up, and going back down to the track, found the negro standing there trying to get another negro to go with him to help get the boat out of the river. They were gone about three hours or more, when I said to Alex that I believed I would go over where they were and take a look at the boat, which I did, and fond it to be a very neat little skiff about sixteen feet long. When the negroes came back with the boat, and while coming through the water towards us, I walked up to Alex and told him to let two of the other men go, as they said they were good swimmers and good boatmen. His reply was: 'No, Bob, it is safe enough, as Thornton and myself have rowed down the river many a time. Let's you and I go on, as it will take at least two hours to cross that place, and if we wait for anyone else we will be in the night, but if we go across now we can attend to all of our business this evening, as Thornton and I are going up the river to McBurney tomorrow and row down it,' and immediately after making this statement he stepped into the boat and walked across to the front and sat down, and turning to me asked, 'Are you going?' My reply was, 'If you are going, I am going too,' and I immediately took my place in the center of the boat.

We were at this time on the west side of the track, and turning our boat in a southwesterly course we started for an old house that stood about three hundred yards directly west of this dangerous place in the track. When we got within about a hundred yards of the house and about two hundred yards from this opening in the track, the negro who was sitting in the back of the boat paddling, dropped his paddle. At this time we were in pretty swift water, and when the paddle was lost it caused the negro who was rowing to get a little excited, and he, in this swift water, commenced digging at his oars for dear life. When he did this I stood up in the boat behind him, and placing my hands on his shoulder and slightly tapping it, I said: 'Keep cool; don't get excited; make every lick count, and though we may not get to the house, yet we will get far enough through this current to allow us to land on the railroad just the other side of this dangerous point.'

At that time he seemed to quiet down, but in a few seconds when the front of the boat turned downstream a little he commenced again, and after making two or three licks in this way dropped his oar on the east side.

When this was done our boat immediately got sidewise in the current and was going very rapidly for the opening in the railroad. I then reached down and got the oar that the negro had laid down, and attempted to paddle out of the heaviest of the current, but in a moment saw that that was impossible, so I took the oar and tried to pole out, but could not touch the bottom of the stream. I then laid the paddle down and told the men in the boat to grab for the railroad right-of-way fence, and not under any circumstances let the boat go beyond that fence.

When we got to the fence we all made a grab for it, but when the boat struck it, it immediately commenced to sink.

At this time Alex was sitting in the front end, apparently paying no attention to what was going on, and the only evidence I have of him hearing what was said was when we got to the fence, he, like the rest of us, tried to grab it.

At the time the boat sank I got up, and taking off my coat and hat, told them all to jump over the fence on the east side, and we all jumped over together about two feet below the fence. We struck in water up under our arms, and very swift, but from some cause we could keep our feet by drifting with the current.

While bobbing around this way Alex came over right close to me, looking for something to get hold of, and took hold of my hand. I then told him that we must not take hold of each other, but that we must get up to the top of the water and swim right through the center of the current.

The negro was at this time going standing upright on through the current, and when he came to the railroad he went under it. I think at this time he was dead.

I got up on top of the water and swam directly through the current over the top of the railroad and over the top of two wire fences, in an easterly direction, passing the right-of-way wire fence on the east side of the track. Then I heard someone hollering, and glancing back, I saw the negro who was following me sitting on the top of the post. I swam on straight east in the current about fifty yards farther, when I saw, off to the right of me, floating on his back with his feet down the stream, the dead negro. I turned southeast towards him. At that time I thought he was an old settler in that country, and knew what he was doing and was aiming to float out, and I thought if he could float out, I could too, but as a fact at that time I had given up all hopes of ever getting out, and realized that it was only a matter of time when I would drown, as I was exhausted from coming through this raging current at the rate of about seventy-five miles per hour. But when I got out to where this negro was, I saw that he was dead, as his mouth was open and the water was streaming into it; then it was I deeply realized that there was not much chance for me to get out, but at the same time I kept swimming, and passed the negro about two feet and turned south and swam about three feet farther, when my left foot struck the ground, and while struggling to get a foothold the dead negro passed me, going on down the stream.

I stood up in the water, and looking back saw Alex, as I thought, sitting on the railroad. I then waded on about twenty yards and stopped to rest, when on looking back again, I saw the negro who was following me get off the post and swim directly to where he had seen me let down and touch bottom.

I then turned, and going on south, waded to a small peach tree, and looking back again saw that the negro who was following me had stopped and was washing his face.

I called to him to come on, and while calling, his father passed me on horseback and went out to him and picked him up and brought him out to a tent on the high ground that I had just passed on my way back to the railroad.

I got on the railroad completely broken down both physically and nervously, and started up the road north to where I thought Alex was sitting, and looking up, called to him to come on and we would go on to Eufaula, but when I looked up I saw that he was standing out in the current about thirty feet from the track to the northwest and about twenty feet from where this terrible current went over and under the railroad, holding to a little sprout not larger than the handle of an umbrella, with three small prongs to it.

I then turned and went back, and, re-wading the water next to the railroad, crossed over to where this negro on horseback had deposited on the ground, as he thought in a dying condition, his son. I asked him to ride to Eufaula and tell all the people that Alex Posey was out here and about to be drowned and to come out and bring about three or four hundred feet of rope. He said he could not get there on horseback. I then told him to come over to the railroad and go on foot. He told me that the man who he had just taken out was his son, and that he was nervously prostrated by the shock, and that he could not possibly walk there.

I then waded back to the railroad and started again to the place where Alex was. When about halfway I met a little negro and asked him to go. He said he had a sore foot and could not possibly walk to the town. I then left him and ran up in about five steps from where the track went into the water. There I came across two negroes sitting down looking at Alex in the water. I asked the first one to go to Eufaula and get men and rope out here to get him out. He said he had the rheumatism and could not go. The second one said he was afraid to cross the river bridge. I then walked by these negroes, and stepping out as close to the water as I could, called to Alex and asked him if he could hold on to that small twig until I could go to Eufaula and get men and rope to get him out.

He looked around over his shoulder and smiling at me, said yes, and with his left hand motioned to me to hurry to town.

I then started back up the track on a run part of the time and part of the time walking as rapidly as possible, and after going about half a mile I came to the river. Running across the bridge, I went up to the water tank and there met John Simpson, Mike Sausman, Jim Wadsworth, and another man who I did not know, and told them what I wanted.

Some men had just taken a boat across to an island to get a man out, and we called them back. With that boat was Mr. W. C. Coppick. We then went down to where Alex was in the water, and Mr. Simpson stepped up and was talking to him to encourage him to hold on a while longer, as we would get him out, while he was himself getting ready to go out in the boat.

Then it was that Mr. Simpson said to me: 'Mr. Howe, you are right; we need plenty of rope; go and tell Jim Wadsworth to go to town after it.'

I ran back through the crowd that had gathered, which consisted of about a dozen men, and saw that Mr. Wadsworth had heard what Mr. Simpson said, and was, with Mike Sausman, running up the track in the direction of Eufaula for the rope.

In the meantime Mr. Coppick and Mr. Simpson had taken the boat out to the fence, but found out they could do nothing until the men came with the rope. After the men had been gone about thirty minutes the train crew came up with about forty Italians. I went to the conductor and asked him if he would run to Eufaula and bring the rope out. He said 'yes,' and, uncoupling the engine from the cars, went back at a rapid rate. In about twenty minutes he came back with about four hundred feet of rope.

Mr. Coppick, Mr. Simpson and a little boy by the name of Pearl Gibson took the rope, and, going out to the fence, tied it to the boat. They could not get to a post directly west of him, but tied it to one so that when the boat was let down it came about five feet to the south and about five feet to the west, leaving Alex standing about five feet to the northeast.

Mr. Coppick went down in the boat, while Mr. Simpson stayed up at the post to hold the boat and the Gibson boy stood at his post to help hold the boat and pull it in. When he got down there, Mr. Coppick got out and attempted to push the boat over to him, then Simpson and Gibson would let it down to him; but the water was so swift that it was impossible to push the boat as much as six inches, so Mr. Coppick got over on the other side and attempted to pull the boat over, but came very near losing his hold on it, and had to get back in.

Mr. Simpson and I then told the men to go out and help with the boat, but at that time there was no one there who could swim but Jim Simpson, and he immediately commenced taking off his clothes to go in, and at the same time Jay Smith was getting ready to go in with him.

In the meantime Alex had requested Mr. Coppick to hand him one end of the rope and he could pull him in. Before doing this Mr. Coppick asked him if he was scared, and he said no. He then asked him if he was excited and he again said no. Then Mr. Coppick handed him one end of the rope, at the same time telling him not to turn loose that twig unless he was sure he could hold the rope. He said he could. Mr. Simpson then called to him not to turn loose of the twig unless he could hold the rope, and added: For God's sake, Alex, don't do it.' He at that time had hold of the rope with his left hand, but was holding the twig with his right. He then told Mr. Simpson that he could hold the rope, and then at the same time he took hold of it with his right hand.

When he did the swift current threw him out in the stream directly behind the boat about four feet, but he still stood on his feet.

Mr. Coppick asked him if he could pull in. He said yes, and attempted to pull himself into the boat, but as he made the pull his feet flew out from under him and left him dragging behind the boat. He then raised his head and told Mr. Coppick that he could not pull himself into the boat.

Jim Simpson then started out to the fence to get to the rope and go down to him, but before he could get to the fence Alex had requested Mr. Coppick to pull him in. Mr. Coppick told him to hold the rope and he would pull him in or pull out the back end of the boat. When he made the pull, Alex's hands began to slip from off the rope. He then turned his head and looked toward the bank where we were standing, and turning and looking back down the stream towards this awful current that was going over and under the railroad track, he opened his hands and passed out of sight for the moment under the railroad.

I saw him for a moment on the east side, apparently dead, as I thought; then his body shot down the stream for the right-of-way wire fence, and there it sank from my sight and I saw him no more.

A word here in regard to this water. The river at this place formed a horseshoe; on the west side of the track there was about three miles square of water, and about the same on the east. The water had broken through the track, leaving a space of about thirty feet, and going through this on a four-foot fall in a distance of about one hundred yards, the track was bent down, leaving the water to run about twelve inches over the top of it and about eight feet under it, with some of the ties hanging down, and the bend in the railroad making the water that ran over it run in a channel about three feet wide, and was so swift that when you threw in a sack of sand it would go down the current about ten feet or more. To strike any portion of that railroad was instant death, so you can readily see that it was an impossibility for or anyone to go in to where he was to attempt to let him come out on a rope, or to lasso him and drag him out, but the only way to possibly save him was to put three good men with a boat and at least fifteen men up at the fence to pull the boat in.

This is the true story of the awful death of the greatest Creek Indian of this country, the most polished newspaper man in the State, and a writer of prose and poetry whose equal in his line we have never known."

XI

The poems of Posey always appeared over the *nom de plume* CHINNUBBIE HARJO. Chinnubbie Harjo, in the Muscogee mythology, had changed character and was regarded as the evil genius of the Creeks. In his original conception he had been their hero, a mighty man endowed with a supernatural powers, but burdened with many of the foibles, limitations, and weaknesses of humanity. He was to the ancient Creeks what Hiawatha was to the Iroquois—what Manabozho was to the Algonquins. Posey seems to have accepted him in his modified capacity, for I find four articles or stories written by him of Chinnubbie. These were doubtless written while Posey was at Bacone University and published in the Instructor. I find them in pamphlet form, and they bear the following titles:

"Chinnubbie Harjo, The Evil Genius of the Creeks,"—
"Chinnubbie Scalps the Squaws,"—
"Chinnubbie's Courtship,"—
"Chinnubbie and the Owl."

The portrayal of Chinnubbie Harjo by Posey seems to assign him to the place which in the ancient lore of the Creeks I have indicated. Pagan religions usually concerned themselves much more with the conciliation of evil spirits than in the discovery and adoration of beneficent ones.

The *nom de plume* was a good one, euphonious and flowing, pleasant to the ear, and genuinely Indian. After his graduation Posey published no poem, that I have found, over any other name; but it seems not to have been his purpose to conceal his identity, for it was generally known that these poems were written by him.

XII

Posey was a striking character—swarthy, as Indians are, erect, and of fine presence. Toward strangers he maintained an impenetrable reserve, and reticence was habitual with him. But to friends—those who had won a place in his heart—his greetings were warm and his manner cordial and gracious. By nature he was gentle, kind, considerate. He was modest in reference to his talents, and he was fully aware of his deficiencies. He did not take every friend to his soul, but some he did. They were usually those who loved literature as he loved it. These were his joy, his constant delight. Their coming kindled happiness, and they were not long with him until he was reading with them and discussing some favorite author. He rarely referred to his own productions, and when he did so it was in disparaging terms.

Posey was the best known man in the Five Civilized Tribes, and was universally spoken of "Alex" Posey. This name he preferred. Indeed, he used no other, even when signing legal documents. He disliked the name "Lawrence," and while it was his name, he never used it. To the Constitution of the State of Sequoyah is signed the favorite form of his name, Alex Posey.

In his home life Posey found true happiness. As a husband he was devoted and affectionate. As a father he was loving and indulgent. By temperament he was never exacting, but always appreciative. He possessed the generous nature of the Indian and was a free spender of money for the comfort of those near and dear to him. While not improvident, he did not comprehend the full value of money. He was very considerate of his family, and if he had five minutes to spare he would take down some favorite volume and read to his wife. His children, a son and a daughter, were his companions. When he was absent from home his family received from him an affectionate letter every day.

XIII

Indians are poetical in their conceptions of life and nature. As observers of the habits of animals and the phenomena of nature they surpass all other people. They are orators by instinct, and no more eloquent people ever lived. Speaking of this characteristic of his people, Posey said:

> "All of my people are poets, natural-born poets, gifted with wonderful imaginative power and the ability to express in sonorous, musical phrases their impressions of life and nature. If they could be translated into English without losing their characteristic beauty and flavor, many of the Indian songs and poems would rank among the greatest productions of all time. Some of them are masterpieces. They have a splendid dignity, gorgeous word-pictures, and reproduce with magic effect many phases of life in the forests—the glint of the fading sunshine falling on the leaves, the faint stirring of the wind, the whirring of insects—no detail is too small to escape their observation, and the most fleeting and evanescent impressions are caught and recorded in most exquisite language. The Indian talks in poetry; poetry is his vernacular—not necessarily the stilted poetry of books, but the free and untrammeled poetry of Nature, the poetry of the fields, the sky, the river, the sun and the stars. In his own tongue it is not difficult for the Indian to compose,—he does it instinctively; but in attempting to write in English he is handicapped. Words seem hard, form mechanical, and it is to these things that I attribute the failure of the civilized Indian to win fame in poetry."

Posey overcame the difficulties of which he speaks and of which he was painfully conscious, and which required tremendous effort and infinite patience and perseverance, for he was a complete Indian. He inherited little from the white man. That which he had from us was mostly acquired. He belonged to a people but two or three generations removed from barbarism. But inherent in his soul was the aspiration to commune with the infinite.

The emotions which stirred him he recorded for us. He was the Apostle of Nature. As long as men are moved by the beautiful in nature they will read the words and bless the memory of this bard of the Creeks—the poet of America's aboriginal people.

XIV

I forego the temptation to enter here upon an analysis of Posey's work.

Every reader may do that for himself.

It has been said that Posey had no faith in a future life. It is impossible that this could be true. Of all people, the Indians are strongest in their faith in a Supreme Being and a future life. Posey was too broad a man to attempt to set bounds to Omnipotence.

To him a Creator was so much in evidence every time he lifted his eyes to behold the beauties of the world and the heavens, that to his mind no argument was required to prove His existence. That his road was full of reverence for the Supreme Architect of the universe will be plain to all who may read what he has said. In his heart he could find no response to the theory that God was best sought and only found by adherence to sects and denominations.

Posey's conception was that God is best served and most reverently worshipped by our expression of the gratitude we feel for the beauties and blessings He so bounteously pours out for us every day. This conception inspired in Posey love for a life which was right and a deep reverence for God as He manifests Himself to His children by his beneficence and the beauties of His handiwork. In this Posey was devout. In it he found the hope of resurrection and a new life—

> *"When Death has shut the blue sky out from me,*
> *Sweet Daffodil,*
> *And years roll on without my memory,*
> *Thou'lt reach thy tender fingers down lo mine of clay,*
> *A true friend "still."*
> *Although I'll never know thee till the Judgment Day."*

William Elsey Connelley.
816 Lincoln Street,
Topeka, Kansas, August 11, 1910.

THE POEMS OF
ALEXANDER LAWRENCE POSEY

Song Of The Oktahutchee[1]

Far, far, far are my silver waters drawn;
    The hills embrace me, loth to let me go;
The maidens think me fair to look upon,
    And trees lean over, glad to hear me flow.
Thro' field and valley, green because of me,
I wander, wander to the distant sea.

Thro' lonely places and thro' crowded ways,
    Thro' noise of strife and thro' the solitude.
And on thro' cloudy days and sunny days,
    I journey till I meet, in sisterhood,
The broad Canadian,[2] red with the sunset,
Now calm, now raging in a mighty fret!

On either hind, in a grand colonnade,
    The cottonwoods rise in the azure sky,
And purple mountains cast a purple shade
    As I, now grave, now laughing, pass them by;
The birds of air dip bright wings in my tide,
In sunny reaches where I noiseless glide.

O'er sandy reaches with rocks and mussel—
    shells,
Blue over spacious beds of amber sand,
By hanging cliffs, by glens where echo dwells—
    Elusive spirit of the shadow-land—
Forever blest and blessing do I go,
A'wid'ning in the morning's roseate glow.

Tho' I sing my song in a minor key.
    Broad lands and fair attest the good I do;
Tho' I carry no white sails to the sea,
Towns nestle in the vales I wander thro';
And quails are whistling in the waving grain,
And herds are scattered o'er the verdant plain.

---

1. Oktahutchee: Okta, sand; Hutchee, river.—A name given to the beautiful North Canadian by the Creek Indian.
2. The South Canadian.

Flowers

When flowers fade, why does
    Their fragrance linger still?
Have they a spirit, too,
    That Death can never kill?
Is it their Judgment Day
    When from the dark, dark mould
Of April and of May
    Their blooms again unfold?

When Love Is Dead

Who last shall kiss the lips of love, when love is
    dead?
Who last shall fold her hands and pillow soft
    her head?
Who last shall vigil keep beside her lonely bier?
I ask, and from the dark, cold height without,
    I hear
The mystic answer: "I, her mother, Earth,
    shall press
Her lips the last, in my infinite tenderness."

To A Daffodil

When Death has shut the blue skies out from
    me,
    Sweet Daffodil,
And years roll on without my memory,
Thou'lt reach thy tender fingers down to mine
    of clay,
    A true friend still,
Although I'll never know thee till the Judgment
    Day.

My Fancy

Why do trees along the river
 Lean so far out o'er the tide?
Very wise men tell me why, but
 I am never satisfied;
And so I keep my fancy still,
 That trees lean out to save
The drowning from the clutches of
 The cold, remorseless wave.

To A Robin

Out in the golden air,
    Out where the skies are fair,
I hear a song of gladness,
    With never note of sadness.
Sing out thy heart's delight,
    And mine of every sorrow.
Sing, sweet bird, till the night,
    And come again tomorrow.

THE DEW AND THE BIRD

There is more glory in a drop of dew,
 That shineth only for an hour,
Than there is in the pomp of earth's great Kings
 Within the noonday of their power.

There is more sweetness in a single strain
 That falleth from a wild bird's throat,
At random in the lonely forest's depths,
 Than there's in all the songs that bards e'er
 wrote.

Yet men, for aye, rememb'ring Caesar's name.
 Forget the glory in the dew,
And, praising Homer's epic, let the lark's
 Song fall unheeded from the blue.

Husse Lotka Enhotulle
(The West Wind)

From o'er the hills it comes to me,
    The clouds pursuing,
With song of bird and drone of bee,
    So soft and wooing;

From o'er the woods, thro' shade and sheen,
    With fragrance teeming,
From o'er the prairies, wide and green,
    And leaves me dreaming.

Across the fields of corn and wheat
    In valleys lying.
It seems to sing a message sweet
    Of peace undying.

I shout aloud—the wildwoods ring
    As they have never—
"Blow, O Wind of the West, and sing
    This song forever!"

Bob White

Bob—Bob White!
The joyous call falls like a silver chime;
And back across the fields of summer-time,
The echo, faint but sweetly clear,
Falls dying on the listening ear—
　　Bob—Bob White!

And when the cheery voice is dead,
　　And silence woos the wind to rest
Among the oak boughs overhead,
　　From valley, hill, or meadow's breast,
There comes an answering call—
　　Bob—Bob White!

And, once more, over all.
The golden Silence weaves her spell,
　　And light and shadow play

At hide-and-seek behind the high
　　Blue walls around the day.

A speck of brown adown the dusty pathway
runneth he,
Then whirreth, like a missile shot, into a neigh-
b'ring tree.
Again, from where the wood and prairie meet.
Across the tasseled corn and waving wheat,
Awakening many tender memories sweet—
　　Bob—Bob White!

Brook Song

If you'll but pause and
    Listen, listen long,
There are far-off voices
    In a wee brook's song,
That come as voices
    Come from out the years;
And you will dream you
    Hear the voice once Hers,
Perhaps, and wend on,
    Blinded by your tears.

On Piney

Far away from the valley below,
Like the roar in a shell of the sea
Or the flow of the river at night,
Comes the voice strangely sweet of the pines.

Snowy clouds, sometimes white, sometimes dark,
Like the joys and the sorrows of life,
Sail above, half becalmed in the blue;
And their cool shadows lie on the hills.

Here and there, when the leaves blow apart,
To admit sunny winds seeking rest
In the shade with their burden of sweets,
Piney Creek shimmers bright, with a cloud

Or a patch of the sky on its breast;
Here the din and the strife of the mart
And the gabble of lips that profane
Are heard not, and the heart is made pure.

In Tulledega

Where mountains lift their heads
    To clouds that nestle low;
Where constant beauty spreads
    Sublimer scenes below;

Where gray and massive rocks
    O'erhang rough heights sublime;
Where awful grandeur mocks
    The brush, and poet's rhyme,

We saw the evening blush
    Above the rugged range,
We heard the river rush
    Far off and faint and strange.

To Wahilla Enhotulle
(To The South Wind)

O Wind, hast thou a sigh
    Robbed from her lips divine
Upon this sunbright day—
    A token or a sign?

Oh, take me, Wind, into
    Thy confidence, and tell
Me, whispering soft and low,
    The secrets of the dell.

Oh, teach me what it is
    The meadow flowers say
As to and fro they nod
    Thro' all the golden day.

Oh, hear, Wind of the South,
    And whispering softer yet,
Unfold the story of
    The lone pine tree's regret.

Oh, waft me echoes sweet
    That haunt the meadow glen—
The scent of new-mown hay,
    And songs of harvest men;

The coolness of the sea
    And forests dark and deep—
The soft reed notes of Pan,
And bleat of straying sheep.

Oh, make me, Wind, to know
    The language of the bee—
The burden of the wild
    Bird's rapturous melody;

The password of the leaves
    Upon the cottonwood;
And let me join them in
    Their mystic brotherhood.

On Viewing The Skull And Bones Of A Wolf

How savage, fierce and grim!
　　His bones are bleached and white.
But what is death to him?
　　He grins as if to bite.
He mocks the fate
That bade, "Begone."
There's fierceness stamped
　　In ev'ry bone.

Let silence settle from the midnight sky—
Such silence as you've broken with your cry;
The bleak wind howl, unto the ut'most verge
Of this mighty waste, thy fitting dirge.

WHENCE

Whence come these sweet æolian airs
Which, in the poet's inmost soul,
Awaken silent melodies?
I ask a wild rose blooming far
Afield, and thus it answered me:
"From places like to this, where love
Abides to start them with his breath."
I questioned then a stately tree,
With leaves a-ripple in the breeze.
"From lonely woods," it gave reply,
"Where Sorrow broods uncomforted."
And then I asked a meadow-lark,
A-bobbing on the waving grass,
As quick, as blithe, its answer came:
"From meadows where I meet the Sun,
And brown bees rove in quest of sweets."
The Tulledega, lying like
A purple shadow in the west,
Gave answer to my question, thus:
"From heights where stormy Passion speaks
In the language of the tempest."

Spring In Tulwa Thlocco

Thro' the vine-embowered portal blows
    The fragrant breath of summer-time;
Far, the river, brightly winding, goes
    With murmurs falling into rhyme.

It is spring in Tulwa Thlocco now;
    The fresher hue of grass and tree
All but hides upon the mountain's brow
    The green haunts of the chickadee.

There are drifts of plum blooms, snowy white,
    Along the lane and greening hedge;
And the dogwood blossoms cast a light
    Upon the forest's dusky edge.

Crocus, earliest flower of the year,
    Hangs out its starry petals where
The spring beauties in their hiding peer,
    And red-buds crimson all the air.

On The Capture And Imprisonment Of Crazy Snake, January, 1900

Down with him! Chain him! Bind him fast!
    Slam to the iron door and turn the key!
The one true Creek, perhaps the last
    To dare declare, "You have wronged me!"
Defiant, stoical, silent,
    Suffers imprisonment!

Such coarse black hair! Such eagle eye!
    Such stately mien!—How arrow-straight!
Such will! Such courage to defy
    The powerful makers of his fate!
A traitor, outlaw,—what you will,
    He is the noble red man still.

Condemn him and his kind to shame!
    I bow to him, exalt his name!

Shelter

In my cabin in the clearing,
    I lie and hear the autumn shower falling
    slow;

Afar, almost out of hearing,
    I lie and hear the wet wind thro' the forest go.

Sense of shelter steals o'er me;
    Into the evening dimness failing,
Into the night before me,
    I lie and fancy I am sailing.

All night the wind will be blowing;
    All night the rain will slowly pour;
But I shall sleep never knowing
    The storm raps ceaseless at my door.

To The Indian Meadow Lark

When other birds despairing southward fly,
    In early autumn-time away;
When all the green leaves of the forest die,
    How merry still art thou, and gay.

O! Golden-breasted bird of dawn.
    Through all the bleak days singing on,
Till winter, wooed a captive by thy strain,
    Breaks into smiles, and spring is come again.

Nightfall

As evening splendors fade
    From yonder sky afar,
The Night pins on her dark
    Robe with a large bright star,
And the new moon hangs like
    A high-thrown scimitar.
Vague in the mystic room
    This side the paling west.
The Tulledegas loom
    In an eternal rest,
And one by one the lamps are lit
    In the dome of the Infinite.

Assured

Be it dark; be it bright;
    Be it pain; be it rest;
Be it wrong; be it right—
    It must be for the best.
Some good must somewhere wait.
    And sometime joy and pain
Must cease to alternate,
    Or else we live in vain.

Trysting In Clover

I laid amid the hum of bumblebees
    And O, and O,
    Above me, to and fro,
The clover-heads were tossing in the breeze!

And O, and O, from meadow, wood or height,
    Afar or near,
    Came sweet the whistle clear,
Athwart the sunny silence, Bob—Bob—White!

The heaven in the south arched low and blue,—
    Too low and blue,
    For clouds to wander thro',
And so they moored at rest as white ships do.

And O, and O, how cool their shadows lay
    Upon the lea,
    In dark embroidery!
How sweet the mock-bird sang, perfect day!

My heart gave answer, Bird, for thee and me,
    O perfect day!
    For she is on her way,
I know, to join me in my reverie!

Between that time and now, lie many years
    And O, and O,
    And O, time changes, so!—
The spring and summer wane and autumn seres.

Sing, Mockingbird, upon the bending bough,
    Sing as of yore!
    My heart responds no more—
She's listening to sweeter music now!

To A Morning Warbler

Sing on, till light and shadow meet,
    Blithe spirit of the morning air;
    I do not know thy name, nor care—
I only know thy song is sweet,
    And that my heart beats thanks to thee,
    Made pure by thy minstrelsy.

To My Wife

I've seen the beauty of the rose,
I've heard the music of the bird,
And given voice to my delight;
I've sought the shapes that come in dreams,
I've reached my hands in eager quest,
To fold them empty to my breast;
While you, the whole of all I've sought—
The love, the beauty, and the dreams—
Have stood, thro' weal and woe, true at
My side, silent at my neglect.

THE IDLE BREEZE

Like a truant boy, unmindful
Of the herd he keeps, thou, idle
Breeze, hast left the white clouds scattered
All about the sky, and wandered
Down to play at leap-frog with the
Grass, and rest in the branches;
While, one by one, the white clouds stray
Apart, and disappear forever.

COME

Above,
The stars are bursting into bloom,
My love;
Below, unfolds the evening gloom.
Come, let us roam the long lane thro'
My love, just as we used to do.

The birds
Of twilight twitter, sweet and low,
And fly to rest, and homeward go
The herds.
Come, let the long lane lead us as it will,
My love, a-winding thro' the evening still.

Behold
How now the full-blown stars are spread,
Like large white lilies, overhead!
But fold
They must, and fade at gray daylight,
My love; they blossom but at night.

The moon,
My love, uncurls her silv'ry hair,
And June
Spills all her sweetness on the air.
Come, let us roam the long lane thro'
My love, just as we used to do.

My Hermitage

Between me and the noise of strife
    Are walls of mountains set with pine;
The dusty, care-strewn paths of life
    Lead not to this retreat of mine.

I hear the morning wind awake
    Beyond the purple height,
And, in the growing light,
    The lap of lilies on the lake.

I live with Echo and with Song,
    And Beauty leads me forth to see
Her temple's colonnades, and long
    Together do we love to be.

The mountains wall me in, complete.
    And leave me but a bit of blue
Above. All year, the days are sweet—
    How sweet! And all the long nights thro'

I hear the river flowing by
    Along its sandy bars;
Behold, far in the midnight sky,
    An infinite of stars!

'Tis sweety when all is still,
    When darkness gathers rounds
To hear, from hill to hill,
    The far, the wandering sound.

The cedar and the pine
    Have pitched their tents with me,
What freedom vast is mine!
    What room! I What mystery!

Upon the dreamy southern breeze,
    That steals in like a laden bee
And sighs for rest among the trees,
    Are far-blown bits of melody.

What afterglows the twilights hold,
    The darkening skies along!
And O, what rose-like dawns unfold,
    That smite the hills to song!

High in the solitude of air,
    The gray hawk circles on and on,
Till, like a spirit soaring there,
    His image pales and he is gone!

Seashells

I picked up shells with ruby lips
    That spoke in whispers of the sea,
Upon a time, and watched the ships,
    On white wings, sail away to sea.

The ships I saw go out that day
    Live misty—dim in memory;
But still I hear, from far away,
    The blue waves breaking ceaselessly.

A Vision Of June

At last, my white Narcissus is in bloom;
    Each blossom sheds a wondrous fragrance. Lo!
    From over bleak December's waste of snow,
In summer garments, lightly thro' the gloom,
Comes June to claim the truant in my room;
    With her the airs of sunny meadows come,
    And in the apple boughs I hear the hum
Of bees; in all the valleys, brooks resume,
'Twixt greening banks, their mumurous melody;
The sunlight bursts in splendor in the blue,
    And soon the narrow walls confining me
Recede into the distance from my view;
    My spirit in the summer's largeness grows.
    And every thorn is hidden by the rose.

The Homestead Of Empire

Lo! Plain and sky are brothers; peak
    And cloud confer; the rivers spread
At length to mighty seas!
    The soul is lifted up
In room whose walls share God's; wherein
    Empire has staked off a homestead!

Roll on, ye prairies of the West,
    Roll on, like unsailed seas away!
I love thy silence
    And thy mysterious room;
Roll on, ye deserts unconfined,
    Roll on into the boundless day!

Roll on, ye rivers of the West,
    Roll on, through canyons to the seal
Ye chant a harmony
    Whereto free people march!
Roll on, O Oregon, roll on!
    Roll on, thunderous Yosemite!

Ye are the grand-voiced singers of
    The great Republic! Ye echo
Thro' the years the hymn of
    Freedom and of power;
The song of union and of peace
    For aye is in thy troubled flow!

Loom! Loom, ye far cold summits of
    The West! Cloud-girt, snow-crown'd, shine
    on!
Keep watch toward the dawn;
    Keep watch toward the night!
Loom! Loom, ye silent sentinels,
    O'er Freedom's vast dominions!

Move on, world of the Occident,
    Move on! Thy footfalls thro' the globe

Are heard as thou marchest
    Into that larger day
Whose dawn lights up the armored front
    In Cuba and the Philippines.

July

The air without has taken fever;
Fast I feel the beating of its pulse.
The leaves are twisted on the maple,
In the corn the autumn's premature;
The weary butterfly hangs waiting
For a breath to waft him thither at
The touch, but falls, like truth unheeded,
Into dust-blown grass and hollyhocks.

The air without is blinding dusty;
Cool I feel the breezes blow; I see
The sunlight, crowded on the porch, grow
Smaller till absorbed in shadow; and
The far blue hills are changed to gray, and
Twilight lingers in the woods between;
And now I hear the shower dancing
In the cornfield and the thirsty grass.

Gone

Gone! Leaving all her bright
    Hopes scattered, shell-like, on
    The shore of life. Gone! Gone!
Like a white dove in flight.

There hangs the robe she wore
    In matchless harmony
    And perfect purity:
She needs it now no more.

She's but a memory
    Of kind deeds and of
    A life that was all love.
How sweet her rest must be,
Beneath the leaves that fall
    From autumn branches bare
    To slumber with her there,
In answer to her call!

Eventide

Beyond the far-off waves the seagulls cry
    As twilight shades
    The emerald glades
And zephyrs waft the strains of nightbirds nigh;
    Now sinks the sun—
    Its course is run—
    The day is done—
It fades in the gold of the western sky.

Now high, in raven files, the must' ring crows
    Their wings display,
    Thro' ether way,
And transient gleams and saffron bars disclose
    And beauties throng
    The sky along;
    And bugs of song
Now pipe among the vales of dew-kissed rose.

Now Night, on high, her spangled robe unfurls,
    Unveils the moon—
    The silver moon—

The orbs, the milky-ways, the circling worlds;
    Now bright, sublime,
    In clusters shine
    The stars divine,
And 'cross the twinkling void the meteor whirls.

A Rhapsody

Oh, to loiter where
    The sea breaks white
    In wild delight
    And throws her kisses evermore,
    A slave unto the palm-set shore!

Oh, to wander where
    The gray moss clings
    And south wind sings
    Forever, low, enchantingly,
    Of islands girdled by the sea!

Oh, I'll journey back
    Some day; some day
    I'll go away,—
    Forsake my land of mountain pine,
    To win the heart that captured mine!

To The Crow

Caw, caw, caw,
Thou bird of ebon hue,
Above the slumberous valley spread in flight,
On wings that flash defiance back at light,
A speck against the blue,
A-vanishing.

Caw, caw, caw.
Thou bird of common sense.
Far, far in lonely distance leaving me,
Deluded, with a shout of mockery
For all my diligence
At evening.

The Call Of The Wild

I'm tired of the gloom
In a four-walled room;
Heart-weary, I sigh
For the open sky,
And the solitude
Of the greening wood;
Where the bluebirds call,
And the sunbeams fall,
And the daisies lure
The soul to be pure.

I'm tired of the life
In the ways of strife;
Heart-weary, I long
For the river's song,
And the murmur of rills
In the breezy hills;
Where the pipe of Pan—
The hairy half-man—
The bright silence breaks
By the sleeping lakes.

Eyes Of Blue And Brown

Two eyes met mine
    Of heav'n's own blue—
Forgetmenots
    Seen under dew.

My heart straightway
    Refused to woo
All other eyes
    Except those two.

Days came and went
    A whole year thro',
And still I loved
    Two eyes of blue.

But when one day
    Two eyes of brown,
In olive set
    Beneath a crown

Of browner hair,
    Met mine, behold,
The eyes beneath
    The shining gold,

Love-lit and loved
    In days of yore,
Grew dim, and were
    Sky-blue no more!

Twilight

O Twilight, fold me, let me rest within
 Thy dusky wings;
For I am weary, weary. Lull me with
 Thy whisperings,
So tender; let my sleep be fraught with dreams
 Of beauteous things.

The Rural Maid

Said I, "Sweet maid, I do not know your name,
    And you, most sure, a stranger are to me;
But birds sing sweeter for your presence here,—
    My heart is captured by your witchery,

    She fled from me,
    In dread of me.

Said I, "Sweet maid, I did not know your name,
    And you, most sure, a stranger were to me;
But birds sing sadder for your absence here,—
    My heart is broken by your witchery."

The Evening Star

Behold, evening's bright star.
Like a door left ajar
In God's mansion afar,
Over the mountain's crest
Throws a beautiful ray,—
A sweet kiss to the day
As he sinks to his rest.

The Blue Jay

The silence of the golden afternoon
    Is broken by the chatter of the jay,
    What season finds him when he is not gay,
Light-hearted, noisy, singing out of tune,
High-crested, blue as is the sky of June?
    'Tis autumn when he comes; the hazy air,
    Half-hiding like a veil, lies everywhere,
Full of the memories of summer soon
To fade; leaves, losing hold upon the tree,
    Fly helpless in the wintry wind's unrest;
The goldenrod is burning low and fitfully;
    The squirrel leaves his leafy summer rest,
Descends and gathers up the nuts that drop,
When lightly shaken, from the hick'ry top.

When Molly Blows The Dinner-Horn

'Tis twelve o'clock in Possum Flat;
The cabbage steams, and bacon's fat;
The bread is made of last year's corn—
When Molly blows the dinner-horn.

The shadows lengthen north and south;
The water wells up in your mouth;
You're neither sober nor forlorn,
When Molly blows the dinner-horn.

A quiet falls, the smoke curls up
Like incense from a censor cup;
It makes you glad that you were born,
When Molly blows the dinner-horn.

The cur, erstwhile stretched in a snore,
Lays stout siege to the kitchen door;
Nor will he raise it, or be gone,
When Molly blows the dinner-horn.

The Flower Of Tulledega

I know a Tulledegan flower rare
    That lifts between the rocks a blushing face,
And doth with every wind its sweetness share
    That bloweth over its wild dwelling-place,
It gathers beauty where the storms are rough
And clings devoted to the rugged bluff.

Far 'bove its sisters in the vale below,
    It swings its censor like a ruby star,
And thither all the days of summer go
    The mountain bees—fierce knights of love and
    war—
To seal in noontide hour—O hour of bliss!—
Each tender vow of true love with a kiss.

And often, like a beauteous blossom blown
    By careless winds o'er heaven's opal floor,
The Butterfly entreats it, "Be my own";
    And never would in valleys wander more,
Content to hang for aye enchanted there
Beside the frowning summit bleak and bare.

"Come sit with me in my green cedar tent,
    Bright Flower," said Tulledega long ago,
Whilst leaning o'er his lofty battlement,
    And wooed the flower from the vale below.
In vain the Oktahutchee pleaded, "Stay:
    Abide here by my mossy brink alway,"

And flashed on thro' the folded hills. "Abide,"
    The Valley said, "Upon my verdant breast."
    "'Tis bleak and cold up there," the Thrushes
    cried.
    "Nay, nay, I love the Tulledega best,"
Replied the lovely Flower as it went
High up the Mountain's rugged battlement.

"Alas!" the River sighed, and cast a tear

Upon a slender reed; while overhead
A passing cloud cast down a shadow drear
　　Upon the valley green in sunshine spread;
And softly sweet from every feathered throat
To music set, escaped a plaintive note.

A chilling breeze came o'er the forest trees,
　　And all the leafy branches shook with cold;
Stechupco blew such tender melodies
　　As Pan blew from his oaten lute of old,
On fair Arcadia's sunny slopes, when Echo
Loved the youth Narcissus to her sorrow.

Abide, O lovely Flower, in your home
　　Of pine and cedar on the mountain height;
To come and go, as I have come and gone
　　So often before,—let that be my delight.
　　'Tis May, and winds that blow from where you
　　　are,
Tell me you hang now like a ruby star.

Coyote

A few days more, and then
There'll be no secret glen,
Or hollow, deep and dim,
To hide or shelter him.

And on the prairie far,
Beneath the beacon star
On evening's darkening shore,
I'll hear him nevermore.

For where the tepee smoke
Curled up of yore, the stroke
Of hammers rings all day,
And grim Doom shouts, "Make way!"

The immemorial hush
Is broken by the rush
Of armed enemies
Unto the utmost seas.

The Mocking Bird

Whether spread in flight,
    Or perched upon the swinging bough,
Whether day or night,
    He sings as he is singing now,—
Till ev'ry leaf upon the tree
    Seems dripping with his melody!

    Hear him! Hear him!
    As up he springeth—
    As high he wingeth
    From roof or limb!

    If you are sad,
    Go cry it out!
    If you are glad,
    Go laugh and shout!

Hear him! What heart can shut him out?
    He hath a song for every mood,
    For every song an interlude,
To dry the tear or stem the shout !

Whether you work, whether you rest
    Hark! I listen! Hear him sing!
As careless as he builds the nest
    For his mate in the spring!

On A Marble Medallion Of Dante

Close-hooded as a monk;
High-cheeked as a Red Man;
High-nosed as a Hebrew;
Full-lipped as a Greek god.

The character revealed
In this bit of white stone
Is such as is not stamped
Upon a human face
Once in a thousand years.

Verses Written At The Grave Of McIntosh[3]

Oh, carol, carol, early thrush,
    A song
Where Oktahutchee's waters rush
    Along!
In dewy bowers perched to greet
    The dawn,
Sing on, O songster ever sweet,
    Sing on!

And, listening to thy ecstasy,
    Oh, let me fancy that I hear,
    An echo of that voice so dear,
Thrown on the morning air by thee!

An echo of the voice
    Of McIntosh, my friend
And Indian brother, true,
    So true unto the end.

Carol, carol, sing
    O bird of melody;
Say as sweet a thing
    Of him as he of thee!

Blossom, blossom, swing
    Thy flowers lovingly,
Sweet wild rose of spring,
    Here where his ashes lie!

As one by one the cold days pass,
    And Life and Love come on a-wing
    In early sens'ous days of spring,
Creep gently hither, modest grass,

---

3. COL. D.N. MCINTOSH was an influential member of the Creek tribe. His grave is in a little Indian cemetery under big oak trees, near the Oktahutchee.

Concealing every ugly cleft,
And cover up the wreck that's left
    By winter rude and pitiless!
O April beauty, then, come too,
In snow-white bonnet, sister true
    Of charity and tenderness!
Ye oaks that spread broad branches at the
    Wind's behest,
Be thou his monument, the watchers o'er his
    rest!

What I Ask Of Life

I ask no more of life than sunset's gold;
    A cottage hid in songbird's neighborhood,
    Where I may sing and do a little good,
For love and pleasant memories when I'm old.

If life hath this in store for me—
    A spot where coarse souls enter not,
Or strife—I'm sure there cannot be
    On earth a fairer heaven sought.

Autumn

In the dreamy silence
Of the afternoon, a
Cloth of gold is woven
Over wood and prairie;
And the jaybird, newly
Fallen from the heaven,
Scatters cordial greetings,
And the air is filled with
Scarlet leaves, that, dropping,
Rise again, as ever,
With a useless sigh for
Rest—and it is Autumn.

To The Century Plant

Thou art gloriously
Crowned at last with beauty;
And thy waxen blossoms,
Born of nameless patience.
Charm away the desert's
Dreariness, as some great
Truth a benefactor's
Cast in persecution
Sheds splendid glory
In another age.

The Sunshine Of Life

The smile of a mother,
The smile of a father,
The smile of a brother,
The smile of a sister,
    The smile of a sweetheart,
When fondly you've kissed her,
    The moment ere you 'part,
The sweet smile of a wife,
    And the smile of a friend
    Who proves true to the end,
Are the sunshine of life.

To A Snowflake

This is no home for thee,
    Child of the winter cloud,
I question God why He,
    In blessing, has allowed
Thee to escape, unless
    It were to have thee bear
To Earth, in sinfulness,
    A sweet, white pardon there.

Red Man's Pledge Of Peace

I pledge you by the moon and sun,
As long as stars their course shall run,
Long as day shall meet my view,
Peace shall reign between us two.

I pledge you by those peaks of snow
As long as streams to ocean flow,
Long as years their youth renew,
Peace shall reign between us two.

I came from mother soil and cave,[4]
You came from pathless sea and wave,
Strangers fought our battles through,—
Peace shall reign between us two.

---

4. The Creeks have a legend about their having originated from the caves and earth.

To A Common Flower

Thy waxen blooms of yesterday
Today all wither and decay,
But, oh, so sweet a life is thine!
    Never knowing ill words spoken,
    Sorrow of a heart that's broken,
So full of days unlike to mine.

Two Clouds

Away out west, one day,
Two clouds were seen astray.
One came up from the sea,
    Afar unto the south,
And drifted wearily;
    One came out of the north.
Away out west that day,
A town was swept away.

To A Sea Shell

What sea-maid's longings dwell
    Upon thy lips, O Shell,
Washed to my feet from the depths of the sea?
    Listening, I hold thee to my ear,
    But the secret that I would hear
Blends with the ocean's mystery.

In Vain

Blow! O Wind of the sea!
Oh, blow! Until I see
The ship that went away
Sail safe into the bay!
Wind of the sea! Wind of the sea!
What tidings dost thou bring to me?
But there's no reply;
There's no sail in sight;
And the years go by
And her hair grows white.

Memories
(Inscribed To George R. Hall)

What sweet and tender memories—
    What joys and griefs are yours and mine!
Hands rest that smote the iv'ry keys,
    And still, the lips that sang divine.

Dear ones, near ones have wended
    Homeward through the vale of tears;
The voice that charmed has blended
    With the silence of the years.

O'er lips that cannot say,
    O'er hearts that cannot heat,
The sky bends blue today,
    And flowers blossom sweet.

Tho' far apart we've drifted, Hall,
    'Tween you and me there's but a single river
And but a single mountain-wall—
    'Tween Rose and Jim and us, the vast Forever!

On The Hills Of Dawn

Behold, the morning-glory's sky-blue cup
Is mine wherewith to drink the nectar up
That morning spills of silver dew,
And song upon the winds that woo
And sigh their vows
Among the boughs!

Behold, I'm rich in diamonds rare,
And pearls, and breathe a golden air;
My room is filled with shattered beams
Of light; my life is one of dreams,
In my hut on
The hills of dawn.

A Vision Of Rest

Some day this quest
    Shall cease;
    Some day,
    For aye,
This heart shall rest
    In peace.
Sometimes—ofttimes—I almost feel
The calm upon my senses steal,
So soft, and all but hear
The dead leaves rustle near
And sigh to be
At rest with me.
Though I behold
    The ashen branches tossing to and fro,
    Somehow I only vaguely know
The wind is rude and cold.

Ensapahutche
(Gar Creek)

Now complaining and cross,
Through the reeds and the moss
I come down with a roar
To the green fields before,
From the hills of the old Doughty ranch,
From the valleys of pine where I branch,
From the hollows and coves where I lie
In the shade of the precipice high,
Through the days of the unclouded sky.

And I flow,
As I go
Through the hills,
Into rills,
Into many a pool,
Overshadowed and cool,
Where the white lily-bloom
Is a light in the gloom.

Down the slope of the wild mountain-side
Come the grasses athirst to my tide,
By the Cardinal led aright.
Far away, like the roar in the shell of
        the sea,
The sad voice of the pine on the crag
        answers me,
As I fall on the rocks at night.

At The Sirens' Call

I fancy that I sit beside
    The shore of slumbers' phantom sea
And see sweet visions die, and hear
    The siren voices calling me.

Am I a shell cast on the shore
    Of Time's illimitable sea,
To hear and whisper evermore
    The music of Eternity?

Kate And Lou

So wondrous fair are Kate and Lou,
And both return my love so true,
I cannot choose between the two,
And so the rolling years go by,
Nor ever halt to question why
I cannot bring myself to woo
Sweet Kate and not love fair Lou, too.
So wondrous fair are Kate and Lou,
And both return my love so true,
I cannot choose between the two,
And so, as the swift years roll by.
Alike I'll love them till I die;
For I can't bring myself to woo
Fair Lou and not love sweet Kate, too.

Nature's Blessings

'Tis mine to be in love with life,
And mine to hear the robins sing;
'Tis mine to live apart from strife,
And kneel to flowers blossoming—
    To all things fair,
    As at a shrine—
    To drink the air
    As I would wine.
To Love I've built a temple here.
    Beneath the boughs of oak and pine,
Beside a spring that all the year
    Tells of a harmony divine.
    I own no creeds
    Sweet Love beside—
    My spirit's needs
    Are satisfied.

To The Summer Cloud

Ever straying,
Never staying,
    Never resting, e'er an aimless rover.
Wind, Shelley's spirit rise to thee,
Up from the cruel sea;
And dost thou bear it ever thro'
The vast unbounded blue,
Ever ranging,
Ever changing,
    Ever yet the same the wide world over!

Hotgun On The Death Of Yadeka Harjo

"Well so," Hotgun he say,
  "My ol'-time frien', Yadeka Harjo, he
Was died the other day,
  An' they was no ol'-timer left but me."

"Hotulk Emathla he
  Was go to be good Injin long time 'go,
An' Woxie Harjoche
  Been dead ten years or twenty, mayb so.
All had to die at las';
  I live long time, but now my days was few;
'Fore long poke-weed an' grass
  Be growin' all aroun' my grave-house too."

Wolf Warrior he listen close,
  An' Kono Harjo pay close 'tention, too;
Tookpafka Micco he almos'
  Let his pipe go out a time or two.

LOWENA

Blue hills between us lie,
    And rivers broad and deep;
But here, as there, a bird
    Is singing me to sleep,
And love has bridged the mountains blue
    And all the streams between us two.

Kind friends, they bid me stay
    And make their homes my own;
But they cannot be you
    To me, and I'm alone
Amid the music sweet,
    And shall be till we meet.

However kind the friends,
    The scenes however fair,
My heart returns to thee,
    Not happy anywhere
Save when thou art near to share
    Life's light of joy or shade of care.

Drifting Apart

Upon Love's sea, our barques shall sail
    No more together;
The darkening sky and rising gale
    Bring stormy weather.

The cruel Fates, at last, sweetheart,
    Our love must sever,—
Must furl our sails, drift us apart
    For aye and ever.

I pray a sunny port be thine,
    When storm is over;
I know whatever lot be mine,
    I'm still thy lover.

'Tis Sweet

'Tis sweet, so sweet, when work is o'er
      At eve, to hear the voice of love
Shout welcome from the cottage door,
      Embowered on the hill above.

From furrowed field, where all the day
      You toil and sweat for little bread
'Tis sweet to see the child at play
      Drop toys and come with arms outspread.

Earth's Lilies And God's

Earth's starry lilies sink to rest,
    All folded in the mere at night;
But God's slip back, and slumber best
    Sky-hidden in the broad daylight.

To Yahola, On His First Birthday

The sky has put her bluest garment on,
    And gently brushed the snowy clouds away;
The robin trills a sweeter melody,
    Because you are just one year old today.

The wind remembers, in his sweet refrains,
    Away, away up in the tossing trees,
That you came in the world a year ago,
    And earth is filled with pleasant harmonies,

    And all things seem to say,
    "Just one year old today."

To Our Baby, Laughing

If I were dead, sweet one,
    So innocent,
I know you'd laugh the same
    In merriment,
And pat my pallid face
    With chubby hands and fair,
And think me living, as
    You'd tangle up my hair.

If I were dead, loved one.
    So young and fair,
If I were laid beneath
    The grasses there.
My face would haunt you for
    A while—a day, maybe—
And then you would forget,
    And not remember me.

The Deer

From out the folded hills,
    That lie beneath a thin blue veil,
There comes a deer to drink
    From Limbo's waters in the dale.

Then flies he back into
    The hills; and sitting here, I dream
And watch, as vain as he,
    My image lying in the stream.

The Athlete And The Philosopher

In Greece, an athlete boasted once
      That he could outswim anyone.
"So can a goose," remarked a sage,
      With eyes alive with wholesome fun.

The athlete boasted on, "And I
      Can deeper dive than any man."
"So can a bullfrog," said the sage.
      But, heedless still, the fool began,

"And more than that, can higher kick
      Than any living many in Greece."
"And so can any jackass," said
      The sage. The athlete held his peace.

Where The Rivers Meet

Lo! What a vivid picture here,
    Of sin and purity,
Here where the rivers join their
    Floods and journey to the sea.

A dirty, earthly look hath one,
Reflects not back the sky;
But mark you, on the other's tide
    The clouds are passing by!

A Reverie

The sky bends over in a sweet
Forgiveness; earth is filled with light;
And mellow autumn hues, soft winds
That croon of summer lands; and thro'
The brooding stillness comes a strain
Of music, and, as leaves are swept
Upon the river's tide away,
My thoughts drift off and on to God.

In The Moonlit Wood

I dream that it is snowing,
    And, waking, do but find
The moonbeams softly glowing
    Thro' branches intertwined.

LIFERS MYSTERY

I wander by the shore of life,
    Enchanted by the voices from the sea;
Forever trying—like a child—
    In vain, to understand its mystery.

MOTHER AND BABY

Tired at length of crying,
   Laughing, cooing, sighing,
The baby lies so qui't and still,
   Scarce breathing in his sleep;
The mother watches, half-inclined
   To hide her face and weep.

Ingersoll

When love and the fireside inspired,
    Words dropped from his eloquent lips
Like music from the golden lyre
    Swept by Apollo's finger-tips.

WHAT MY SOUL WOULD BE

What mountain glens afar
And woodland valleys are
To echoes in the air,
My soul would be
    To harmony.

An Outcast

Pursued across the waning year,
By winds that chase with lifted spear,
A leaf, blood-stained, fell spent at last
Upon my bosom, poor Outcast!

Sunset

By coward clouds forgot,
    By yonder's sunset glow,
The Day, in battle shot,
    Lies bleeding, weak, and low.

The Haunted Valley

Ever, somewhere in the boundless blue,
    Floats a cloud, like a ship at sea;
Ever a shadow lies on the hills,
    And a wind from the south blows free.

Ever is heard the voice of the pines
    As they weep o'er a long-lost love,
And ever, like the path of a star,
    Flows the stream with hills above.

Ever the glens betray, passing sweet,
    Secrets of brown lovers no more;
Ever the huntsman lingering there
    At eve hears the dip of the oar;

Behold on the moonlit wave afar,
    Two vague forms in a light canoe,
That is lost anon in the shadow
    Where the river bends out of view.

A Vision

In pensive mood she stood,
   In garments white like snow,
Beside the darksome wood,
   Amid the twilight glow;
As if she held communion there
With spirits in the fading air.

And, loath to break the spell—
   The sweet enchantment that
She seemed to love so well—
   I backward slept; thereat,
The beauteous vision fled from me.
In strange and silent mystery.

Morning

The cloud-dikes burst, and lo!
    The night is swept away
And drowned in overflow
    Of Light at break of day!

The Open Sky

I look up at the open sky,
    And all the evils in
My heart the instant pale and die,
    For, lo! I cannot sin!

The Poet's Song

The poet sings but fragments of
A high-born melody—
A few stray notes and castaways
Of perfect harmony
That come to him like murmurs from
The sea of mystery.

Midsummer

I see the millet combing gold
    From summer sun,
In hussar caps, all day;
    And brown quails run
Far down the dusty way,
    Fly up and whistle from the wold;

Sweet delusions on the mountains,
    Of hounds in chase,
    Beguiling every care
    Of life apace,
    Though only fevered air
That trembles, and dies in mounting.

A Simile

Like bits of broken glass,
Chance scatters in the sun,
Our deeds reflect the light
We carry in the world.

June

O maid, of shape divine,
    Who holds, in act to sup,
An over-brimming cup
    Of sensuous sunshine.

A Valentine

Your cheeks are garden-spots
Of Touch-me-nots;
Your hair the gathered beams
Of sunny dreams;
And that your soul looks thro'
Are hits of fallen blue.

No wall hath circled yet,
Nor dews have wet,
A red rose like your lips.
To steal sweet kisses from your brow,
A lightsome zephyr I would be,—
A brook to murmur you a vow
Of love and constancy.

Mount Shasta

Behold, the somber pines have pitched their tents
    At Shasta's base, like hosts of Night;
For aye besieging in his battlements—
    For aye in vain—their monarch, Light!

Though seas dry up and empty deserts bloom;
    Though races come and pass away
From earth, it still, it still is seen to loom,
    And to flash back God's smile for aye!

Frail Beauty

The raven hair of youth turns gray;
    Bright eyes grow dim; soft cheeks grow pale;
The joyous heart becomes less gay:
    For beauty is a thing so frail,
If once Time's fingers touch it in caress,
It droops, and loses all its loveliness.

To A Hummingbird

Now here, now there;
E'er poised somewhere
In sensuous air.
I only hear, I cannot see,
The matchless wings that beareth thee.
Art thou some frenzied poet's thought,
That God embodied and forgot?

MEANINGLESS

Till baby lips have spoken "papa, mama,"
 There is no meaning in the words at all;
The house is but a pile of brick or lumber,
 Till baby feet have pattered thro* the hall.

The Conquerors

The Caesars and the Alexanders were
But men gone mad, who ran about a while
Upsetting kingdoms, and were slain in turn
Like rabid dogs, or died in misery.
Assassins laid in wait for Caesar; wine,
Amid the boasts of victory, cut short
The glory of the Macedonian;
Deception cooled the fever Pompey had;
Death was dealt to Phyrrus by a woman's
Hand; Themistocles and Hannibal drank
Deep of poison in their desolation.

A Glimpse Of Spring

Overcast is the sky,.
And the wind passes by,
    Breathing blight.
Yet, afar in the gloom,
In the desolate room,
    Cold and white,
Where December is king,
I hear a lone bird sing.
    And the gloom,
Ere my glad lips can say,
From the earth melts away,
In the warm smile of Spring,
And the frosty winds bring
    Sweet perfume.
In the vast waste of snow,
I see the roses bloom.

Mother's Song

I hear a distant melody,
    And years come crowding back to me,
Thro' vistas dim of memory.
    As ships to haven from the sea;

Each freighted with the dreams of youth,
    And moor them in the restless bay
About my heart a while, and then
    Each sails away—so far away!

    I hear it ever;
    It ceases never;
    On land and sea
    It follows me,

So soft and low and far away,
    Like echoes dying in the folded hills.
I hear it there, go where I may,
    A cure for all the sad heart's ills.

ODE TO SEQUOYAH

The names of Waitie and Boudinot—
    The valiant warrior and gifted sage—
And other Cherokees, may be forgot,
    But thy name shall descend to every age;
The mysteries enshrouding Cadmus' name
Cannot obscure thy claim to fame.

The people's language cannot perish—nay,
    When from the face of this great continent
Inevitable doom hath swept away
    The last memorial—the last fragment
Of tribes,—some scholar learned shall pore
Upon thy letters, seeking ancient lore.

Some bard shall lift a voice in praise of thee,
    In moving numbers tell the world how men
Scoffed thee, hissed thee, charged with lunacy!
    And who could not give 'nough honor when
At length, in spite of jeers, of want and need,
Thy genius shaped a dream into a deed.

By cloud-capped summits in the boundless
        west,[5]
    Or mighty river rolling to the sea,
Where'er thy footsteps led thee on that quest,
        Unknown, rest thee, illustrious Cherokee!

5. Sequoyah wandered away from his tribe, and died somewhere in the southwest part of the United States or Mexico.

POHALTON LAKE

Thick heavy leaves of emerald lie
 Upon Pohalton's waters blue,
 Overspread with lustrous drops of dew,
Dashed from my oar, as I glide by
 In my swift light canoe.

Large water-lilies, virtue-pure,
 Bright stars that with Pohalton fell
 From heaven where the angels dwell,
Drive back the shadows that obscure,
 And, siren-like, my fancies lure.

Huge frightened turtles disappear;
 And as the ripples widen o'er
 The lake toward the reedy shore,
The dragon-fly, a wise old seer,
 Drops down upon the log to pore—

Unmindful of the moccasin
 That, swift with darting tongue, slips by
 And climbs a sunny drift to dry.
Reposing half awake, his tawny skin
 Scarce revealed to the searching eye.

And, ever and anon, the breeze
 From piney mountains far away,
 Steals in; and waters kiss the day.
And break the image of the trees
 That looking downward, sigh dismay.

The wood spirit[6] is wandering near,
 Wrapt in old legend mystery;
 I drift alone, for none but he
And nature's self are native here
 Of me to know. But now I see

---

6. The Stechupco.

The patient heron by the shore
    Put down his lifted leg and fly,
    While echoes from the woods reply
To each uncanny scream, low o'er
    The lake into the evening sky.
Vast brooding silence crowds around;
    Dark vistas lead my eye astray,
    Among vague shapes beyond the day
Upon the lake, I hear no sound;
    I go ashore, and hasten 'way.

HAPPY TIMES FOR ME AN' SAL

Hear the happy jays a-singin';
    Leaves a-driftin' in the medder;
    See the 'simmons turnin' redder.
An' the farmer boy a-grinnin'
    At his copper toes.

Happy times fer me an' Sal;
Happy times fer Jim an' Al;
We've raised a sumshus crop,
An' we're upon the top,
    In our new-bought clothes.

More an' more it's gittin' cooler;
    Frost is makin' purtier pictures
On the winder-panes. By victers!
I am feelin' like a ruler
    Over all this earth.

Happy times fer me an' Sal;
Happy times fer Jim an' Al;
We've raised a sumshus crop,
An' we're upon the top,
    Settin' by the he'rth.

Nights are havin' longer hours;
    Sleep is surely growin' finer;
    Dreams becomin' sweeter, kin'er,
Since the season of the flowers.
    Winter days fer me.

Lots o' time fer liberal thought;
Lots o' time to worry not,
When snow's knee-deep outdoors,
An' driftin' on the moors,
    Like a silver sea.

DEATH OF A WINDOW PLANT

The air was chill,
The leaves were hushed,
The moon in grandeur
Climbed the spangled
Walls of heaven,
When the angel came
That whispers death;
Unseen, unheard,
To lisp that word, and
Leave my window
Sad when night should
Blossom into day.
The moon had waned,
And each bright star.
Like visions of a
Dream. Up rose the
Sun on wings of
Gold, and soared thro' fields
Of light serene;
All earth seemed gay,
And banished from it
Sorrow; birds sang
Songs of summer
In the clear sweet sky.
But I was sad,
And song of bird
Nor sky of splendor
Could for one brief
Moment bring a
Solace to my heart.
I mourned, and all
Was dark and drear
Within my chamber,
Lorn and bare, where
Sweetness was and,
Beauty for a day.
My window-friend,
I'll dig thy grave

Inter thee grandly
No sod shall lie.
Nor blossom there
Thy kindred flowers.
Within my soul's
Deep core is built
Thy tomb enduring.
Ah, morn shall kiss
Thee nevermore
In purple of dawn;
And stars shall rise
And twinkle in
Vain and pass away.
Should all thy race
Thus disappear,
In death forsake the
Soil in which you
Grew, the world would
Then be sad as I.

Glossary

Crazy Snake.— Chitto Harjo. The leader of a band of Creeks who oppose the abolishment of their tribal rights. Several times Harjo has been imprisoned because of his defying the United States authorities.

Haunted Valley.— A spot in the Tulledega hills along the Oktahutchee. The legend is that the spirits of the lost lovers haunt the valley and stream

Piney.— A Stream in the Tulledega hills.

Sequoyah.—The Cherokee who invented the Cherokee alphabet.

Stechupo.— A legendary being, very tall, who inhabits the woods and blows on a reed. The Indians believe that if you can get a sight of this person, you will become a great hunter.

Tulledega.— Border line. A name given a range of hills lying along the Oktahutchee, west of the poet's home.

Tulwa Thlocco.— A large settlement of people. This settlement lies on the north side of the Oktahutchee.

Note About the Author

Alexander Lawrence Posey (1873—1908) was a Creek journalist, poet, and politician. Born near Eufaula, Posey was the eldest of twelve children of Lewis Henderson Posey and Nancy—Creek name, Pohas Harjo—Phillips Posey. Orphaned early, Posey was collectively raised in the Creek Nation along with his siblings by his mother's Wind Clan in the tribal town of Tuskegee. Leading up to the death of his parents, Posey and his siblings spoke the Muscogee language though their father insisted they learn English, receive somewhat of a formal education, and by some means, assimilate into a more Euro-centric culture. While Posey would develop the ability to read and write in English (going so far as to be inspired by the naturalism of John Burroughs and Henry David Thoreau) he would never forsake his Native heritage, working at the *Indian Journal* throughout his college years and going on to represent his mother's clan in his membership with the Creek National Council. At the age of twenty-eight, Posey gained national recognition for founding the first Native American daily newspaper, the Eufaula *Indian Journal.* Here he would publish letters under the fictional persona of "Fus Fixico," a full-blooded Muscogee traditionalist who would comment in Creek dialect—made popular at the time by Black authors and "Negro dialect"—on the state of Native American and European relations as they pertained to U.S. politics and maintaining a sense of sovereignty in the Native territories. In many ways an activist, Posey would use his position as secretary to the Sequoyah Constitutional Convention to draft a constitution in hopes of establishing an indigenous-controlled State of Sequoyah. The petition would ultimately be rejected by the United States Federal Government, but as one of Posey's last major acts before his untimely death in 1908 it nevertheless cemented his legacy as a leading Native American figure of the early twentieth century.

bookfinity & MINT EDITIONS

Enjoy more of your favorite classics with Bookfinity,
a new search and discovery experience for readers.
With Bookfinity, you can discover more vintage
literature for your collection, find your Reader Type,
track books you've read or want to read,
and add reviews to your favorite books.
Visit www.bookfinity.com, and click on
Take the Quiz to get started.

Don't forget to follow us
@bookfinityofficial and @mint_editions

CPSIA information can be obtained
at www.ICGtesting.com
Printed in the USA
JSHW011547050623
42744JS00004B/64

9 781513 201047